Charles Gleason Elliott

How the Lewis Boys made the Farm pay

Charles Gleason Elliott

How the Lewis Boys made the Farm pay

ISBN/EAN: 9783743344792

Manufactured in Europe, USA, Canada, Australia, Japa

Cover: Foto ©ninafisch / pixelio.de

Manufactured and distributed by brebook publishing software
(www.brebook.com)

Charles Gleason Elliott

How the Lewis Boys made the Farm pay

How the Lewis Boys Made the Farm Pay.

BY "ORMUS."

CHAPTER I.

A CONSULTATION.

It was a dark day for the Lewis family when they re-
turned from performing the last sad rites connected with
the burial of the husband and father. The mother and four
children were left without a counselor and natural helper to
fight the battle of life, which, with the temptations and
business difficulties which are always besetting men, became
a contest of no slight import to the young people of our
time.

Only a year before this event, Abram Lewis had held
an important position in a zinc-smelting establ.   ·t located in a large city in Northern Illinois; and was giving
his family the usual comforts and privileges which a man
with a liberal salary was able to bestow. A service of some
years in this establishment had seriously impaired his health,
and he saw that he must at once relinquish his position
and seek other employment. He accordingly purchased a
farm of eighty acres, located about five miles from the city,
and moved upon it the following spring, expecting that
with the aid of the two boys, who were nineteen and seven-

teen years old respectively, he would be able to cultivate the farm profitably and perhaps regain his health. But the disease which had fastened upon him before leaving the city, retained its hold in spite of wholesome country air and exercise, and before the summer harvests were gathered he was a helpless invalid.

The boys worked faithfully during the summer, being often obliged, however, from lack of knowledge and experience in farming, to watch their neighbors and, in a measure, imitate their operations. The care and work attending the illness of their father also interfered with their farm work, and on the whole, their first year's work was anything but encouraging. The neighbors sometimes volunteered kindly advice, but more often ominously shook their heads, and passed words among themselves to the effect that there was no use of those city boys attempting to make a living by farming.

Now, in mid-winter, the father had passed away, and the family was left with an eighty-acre farm upon which there was a debt of nine hundred dollars. What should they do? was the question uppermost in the mind of each at the opening of our narative.

"We had better sell the farm and stock and go back to the city," said James, the younger of the boys. "George and I can get something to do for which we are better fitted than digging on this poor farm. The land is wet, the barns and fences out of repair, and we have scarcely made a living during the past year. How can we ever expect to make repairs and pay off the debt?"

"For my part," said George, "I don't think much of the city. I've had enough of it, and do not share your hope of getting lucrative employment. The times are hard and the places that we are fitted for are full, and plenty of idle boys waiting to fill any vacancies that may occur. I think that we have learned something about farming this year, even if we have made no money, and we certainly can do better another year. Besides, we have this farm and the stock upon it, which will not now bring at a forced sale as much as father paid for it. 'A bird in the hand is worth two in the bush,' I've read, and I believe we had better stick to the farm. What do you think, mother?"

"My opinion is," said Mrs. Lewis, "that if you and James will be contented and take up the business with a will, we had better stay on the farm. You will have many things to learn, though the experience already gained will save you from a repetition of the mistakes made this year. You both have a good business education, and your younger sisters, Nellie and Alice, can attend the district school with profit for some time yet. We can live here comfortably and happily, and if you succeed with the farm, we can in time pay off the debt."

"I am contented enough," said James, "and I like to work well enough, but I want to make money by working. There's no fun in work unless it pays something."

James was impulsive, ambitious, and in regard to work, much like a colt beginning to plow, always ready to pull as long as everything moves easily, but easily disheartened at difficulties.

A knock was heard at the door, and Uncle John came in. He was one of those uncles which almost every neighborhood has, one whose age and experience had given a fund of wisdom of which all were ready to avail themselves. He was privileged in the matter of giving advice, censure and commendation. While in some things he was more conservative than the spirit of the times approved, yet, he was a safe counselor, and the family were glad to have him drop in at this opportune time. Many times during the past summer had the boys seen Uncle John slowly walking across the farm, cane in hand, towards the distant field in which they were working. He never left without giving them some practical instruction. Uncle John liked to encourage steady, industrious boys, and he thought he saw these qualities in George and James, as he had watched them at various times during the season.

"Well boys," began Uncle John, as he seated himself in the chair offered him by little Alice, "what have you concluded to do? Your father has gone the way of all the earth, and you must fill his place in the family as best you can."

"We think, Uncle John," said Mrs. Lewis, as the boys hesitated, "that we will stay on the farm. The boys think that they can succeed at that better than to attempt anything in the city."

"Very sensible, very sensible," replied the old man, as he leaned forward and with his cane slowly pushed a fugitive lump of coal toward the hearth, "Nothin's made by changin' 'round. If ye can make a sort o'decent livin', stick where you air, and kinder improve and build up. It's slow work improvin' a farm, but there ain't nothin' that pays a surer profit. Now, ye might go West and get land cheap, but as long as you've got a fair sort o' farm here, I don't think you'd make nothin' by the change."

"But the land is so wet. Some of it didn't raise anything last year," said James, "and some of it plowed in the spring like a bag of wool, and some of it was as soft as mush in the spring, and as hard as a board in the summer. I don't see how we can bring any good out of such land."

The impetuous James was quick to observe the weak points of the farm, and their bearing upon the money-making qualities.

"Well now, boys," said the old man, "when you've got such land as that, I suppose you've got to drain it afore it'll do you much good. I never took much stock in this drainin' business until lately. I allus thought that what drainin' Natur' wanted done to her land, she'd do it herself. I found out arter a spell that it seemed to suit Natur' well enough without any more drainin', but if man wanted to cultivate the land Natur' didn't object to his breaking the sod and drainin' the sile, so as to make his work more profitable."

"Now there was my son Clem : He got it into his head that he must drain that south lot ; he'd read suthin' about drainin' somewhere I believe. I told him 'twant no use. 'Twouldn't amount to nothin'. The Almighty had made that south lot wet land, and he'd better quit foolin' with it. But he wanted to do it—he was always ruther contrary, so 1 told him to go ahead and learn by experience, if he wouldn't learn any other way. I declare to goodness if we ain't had a good crop off of that flat every year since it was drained. Since then, I've had considerable faith in drainin' wet land. That's what you'll have to do boys; or it won't pay you to work some o' that wet land o' yours. 'Tain't so very new either, this drainin' work, as I found out since. We sometimes think a thing is new because we never saw it nor tried it."

The boys looked interested, surprised and not a little mystified. They knew nothing of drainage, except as they had heard it mentioned occasionally by the neighbors, and then it appeared to them as a far-off impractical thing.

"But about the repairing business of the farm?" broke forth the irrepresible James. "We don't know how to fix fences or repair implements, and so everything will soon go to rack. We are about as ignorant as babies."

"All a fellow needs is a little gumption. 'Twon't take ye long to learn to use tools so ye can knock together a gate and hang it, and patch up things generally so that they will look respectable like. Ye don't want to run to town every time ye break something. Learn to fix it yourself."

"How can we learn?" said James.

The old man looked at James, then at his mother, and finally bringing his cane down on the floor with a thump, said: "Look here! I reckon you'll be quick to learn how to handle the tools. You come over to our farm, where we have a kind of a shop, and Clem will teach you. Clem's right handy with tools, and if you want to learn pretty bad, you can pick up a good many things by being with him a spell."

"O thank you," said James; "I'll try it, and maybe we can yet learn to run the farm in fine style."

George, the slower and steadier of the two had some inward misgivings as to the stability of his brother James' purpose, but he offered no discouraging word. What had been said had merely started a train of thought in his mind, from which plans might be developed and ultimately carried into execution. His naturally careful methods of thought and work were in his favor for filling the place of head worker and thinker on the farm; and though he was young and inexperienced, he was ready to learn by precept, and quick in observation.

Uncle John after a few more words of advice, left the family with clearer ideas of the course necessary to pursue. The boys, though they had no plans laid, were encouraged, and looked forward to their work with pleasure.

Courage and pluck accomplish great things in the practical affairs of life.

CHAPTER II.

THE BOYS GO TO A FARMERS' INSTITUTE.

For several days after Uncle John's visit, the boys and the "little mother," as George sometimes called her, commented upon his advice, talked over their resources and canvassed the value and probable income of what they had on hand. Happily there was no debt except the nine hundred dollars yet due upon the farm which, if the annual interest were paid would not mature for five years.

James was enthusiastic over the prospect of learning farm

mechanics. His first lesson in Clem's work-shop in no way dampened his ardor, but rather increased his desire to learn. The many useful things which James saw, all neatly made by his teacher, created in him a desire to equal them by the exercise of his own skill. He now spent a portion of each day with Clem, and was acquiring skill in the use of common wood-working tools.

Two weeks had passed, and James came to supper one evening with something concealed under his overcoat, an expression of mingled pride and pleasure on his face.

What are you holding under your coat?" called out Nellie "A little dog?   Let me see it quick !"

"No; it's something for mother," replied James; and he uncovered a neatly made box to be used in polishing table-kuives. "Here," explained he, "is the inclined block to lay the knives on when you rub them, here is the cork to rub them with, and here is the place for the scouring brick. All my own work, mother. I saw the plan and description of it in the 'Farmer.' "

"Indeed," said the mother, taking the box and looking at it carefully, "You have done nicely, you are quite a mechanic. These joints are neatly made. I think we must get a few tools so that you can have a work shop at home."

The box was examined in turn by George, Nellie and Alice, and as they sat down to the supper table, James entertained them with a description of some of Clem's work which he had seen, and assured them that he knew that he could do as well after he had practiced as long. The appreciation of the family had raised his hopes of success to the highest pitch.

The skill to use tools does not in itself make a successful workman. There must be a certain amount of inventive genius combined with practical judgment, which must be so applied that the result of the work will serve the intended purpose. A structure may be well made, yet the adjustment and strength of the separate parts may be so ill suited to their office as to make the whole worthless. James had much more to learn than he supposed, yet, as good courage and enthusiasm are half the battle, he certainly was on the road to success.

In the meantime George had been busy taking special care of the live stock, and studying carefully the back numbers of the "Farmer," the agricultural paper his father had subscribed for the spring before. The "little mother" had looked them over and marked such items as she thought would be instructive, not failing to read many things herself that might eventually prove useful to her as commander-in-chief of the farm.

One cold morning as George was about the barn a stranger drove into the yard.

"Hello! good morning," said the stranger, as he saw George emerge from the crib with a basket of corn. "Is this where the Lewis family lives?"

"Yes, sir;" replied George. "Come into the house and warm yourself, you must be cold."

"Thank you, I'm not cold. My name is Allen. I heard that the boys here were young in the farming business, and go-ahead sort of fellows, and I thought I'd stop and tell you that we are going to hold a Farmers' Institute at Dempsy's

Hall next week, and would like to have you attend. There'll be addresses and discussions upon subjects interesting to all of us farmers. You'll find the meeting an interesting one, and it'll be strange if you don't find it a profitable one to you in more ways than one. Be sure and come if you can."

George thanked Mr. Allen and added that he and his brother would try and attend. He remembered having heard that Mr. Allen had been a member of the State Legislature, and was now a prominent farmer in an adjoining township. George felt flattered by a personal call from a man so much esteemed in the community, as well as pleased that he should have taken so much interest in them all as to invite him to a meeting of intelligent farmers.

The time appointed for the meeting of the Institute found George and James at Dempsy Hall, which was in the village of Brooktown, about four miles distant from the Lewis farm. Mr. Allen introduced them to several farmers who were about the fire chatting familiarly upon current topics before the meeting was called to order. The boys came to listen and learn, and so merely, in answer to the questions of the farmers, told who they were, and where they lived, and what they wanted to do.

The programme was full and the time well occupied by interesting papers and lectures. One address made by Mr. Allen upon "The Young Farmers' Training" seemed just adapted to the needs of the boys at this time.

"Don't think," said he, "that a school education makes a good farmer, even if that education is obtained at an agricultural college. It is only the foundation upon which a practical farmer should build. I would rather risk the chances of success with the uneducated boy who has the faculty of seizing upon and appropriating the information he may happen to pick up, than with the educated young man who cannot make use of his acquired knowledge. The business man's motto should be : 'Make the best use of what you have.' Be thorough, be practical. Get all the education you can, but make use of it. Learn principles and apply them. Read good books, be industrious, preserve your health, and use both head and hands."

"These were some of the points that George managed to take down in his note book, and which helped him remember many other things said in connection with them.

"What books relating to the farm would you recommend?" some one asked.

"A few of the many good ones," replied Mr. Allen, "are : 'Todd's Young Farmers' Manual,' 'The Soil of the Farm,' 'Coburn's Swine Husbandry,' 'Downing's Rural Essays,' 'Harris' Talks on Manures,' and 'Our Farmers' Account Book.'"

The boys were invited to take dinner with Mr. Allen's family, only half a mile away. While waiting a few minutes for dinner to be announced they were entertained by a daughter of the family ; to whom James soon began to relate some of his ludicrous experiences in learning the use of tools."

"I tried a new project last year," said Miss Allen, "and succeeded very well."

"You! What was it ?" said James.

"Starting plants in hot-beds," said the lady. "My brother made the frames and arranged the beds, and I attended to them after that, and sold the plants for early setting. I sold thirty dollars' worth of plants. The frames cost us only five dollars, so that we got twenty-five dollars for our work, which, considering that most of it was girl's work, did very well; at any rate that is what father says."

"That's jolly," said James. "How do you make the beds and manage the work?"

Dinner was announced which cut short the description of the hot-bed which Miss Allen was about to give.

"I'll find out more about that hot-bed business," thought James. "It strikes me that there is something in it. I'll ask that brother of hers about it if I get a chance."

In the afternoon land drainage was one of the topics to be treated; and as Uncle John's talk to the boys had excited their interest in this subject by telling them that if they wanted to make their farm pay they must drain it, they gave close attention to what was said.

The speaker who introduced the subject gave his own experience in draining a wet part of his farm, together with some of the details of the work, and the principles which govern the results.

"There," thought George, "Mr. Durand's farm is much like ours. That talk hits our case exactly."

"Mr. Chairman," said Uncle Dan Murry, a middle aged man in the back part of the hall, "I'd like to say something on this subject. I've farmed a good many years without any of this drainage stuff getting into my bill of fare; and if anybody here has raised more corn and hogs than I have,

or has made more money than I have, I'd like to see him.
There are a good many things in this drainage business that
I don't understand, and a good many things stated by the
gentleman who opened this subject that I don't believe.
When I was a boy the old topers were accustomed to say
that they drank whisky in summer to keep them cold and
in winter to keep them warm; but I know to-day, and so do
you, that its bosh. They wanted to drink and were bound
to have it, that's all. You drainage folks talk about the way
the topers did. You say that you drain in a wet time to
make the soil dry, and in a dry time to make the soil moist.
And then talk about a drained soil being warmer than a wet
one. May be you think I don't know anything about science. I know this : that black colored things draw the heat
more than those of light color. A wet soil is blacker than
a dry one and so draws the heat more and must be warmer.
Why, in summer after a shower of rain has fallen upon
a cornfield and the sun comes out warm again, that field will
steam like a kettle of hot potatoes. That shows that the
wet soil is drawing heat from the sun right into it. I tell
you you're all crazy on this drainage. You've been led
around by the nose by the ditchers, dealers, tile makers, and
I don't know who all, until you're all bent on digging your
money into the ground instead of out of it. I believe in
sticking to the old way."

"Farmers don't all agree any more than other people,"
thought George. "I believe that I know enough about Natural Philosophy to see where Uncle Dan is wrong and why
Mr. Durand is right."

The number of farmers that rose to their feet ready to answer the statements of Mr. Murry and to add their observation upon the subject soon showed that Uncle Dan was mistaken in practice and science as he chose to call it. At least George came to the conclusion that the weight of evidence was in favor of draining wet land.

That evening the boys recounted the events of the day to the "little mother" and sisters. Nor did James forget to relate the conversation with Miss Allen about the hot-bed scheme, and how she had succeeded.

CHAPTER III.

PLANS AND DIFFICULTIES.

The winter was soon gone and the early spring rains dispelled all traces of wintry fetters and gave promise of another seed time and harvest. The boys continued to occupy themselves busily with plans and work for the coming season. James had now arranged a workshop in the barn and evidences of his handiwork began to appear about the premises.

The plan that had been uppermost in George's mind since he heard the discussions at the Farmer's Institute, was to drain their little farm, or at least to make a beginning. He well knew that they had but little money for any purpose and none with which to begin his cherished project. If he had only a hundred dollars he thought that he could make a very good beginning. They had a fine colt which in another year would make a good farm horse and a neighbor had offered a hundred dollars for him. Should they sell? After a family consultation it was decided to sell the colt and invest the proceeds in the drainage.

A brief description of the Lewis farm should here be given in order that the reader may enter into, and understand, the project that our young friends were about to undertake. As before intimated, the farm contained 80 acres being in the usual form of Western farms of that size, one half mile long and a quarter mile wide. The buildings were at the north end on the only public road that bordered it. It had always been called the "flat eighty," and within the last twelve years had been owned by four different men and all of them had sold out and moved away poorer than when they came, Uncle John had told the boys. A depression or slough extended the entire length of the eighty acres, through the center of which was a shallow, open ditch, cut there by some former owner but now nearly closed. This slough was the natural outlet for the drainage water of the entire farm and passed not far from the barn across the public road and discharged into a large ditch in a neighbor's farm; connecting with this main and slough were side depressions or draws, leading from one or another pond and flat or sag. The farm was thus divided into small irregular fields which were cultivated at great disadvantage not only by reason of their smallness and irregular shape, but also because the so called dry land was often too wet for the growth of the common cereals. The soil was a rich, black, prairie loam and seemed to produce corn, oats and grass in great abundance, when in the proper condition. The subsoil was a retentive clay, so that the surplus water must pass off by surface drainage or by evaporation.

George had gone down to the culvert at the road just after a spring rain and was watching the water of his farm pour through the culvert and then spread out over the flat below on his neighbor's farm.

"Would a tile drain carry the water now coming off the farm?" thought he, "and if there were a drain there three feet below the surface where could the water be discharged? I don't believe I know much about this business after all."

As he was about to turn away he saw Mr. Allen riding toward him, and waited till he came within speaking distance. "You're just the man I want most to see," said George, after the greetings were over; "We want to begin draining our farm this spring. The outlet for the whole, is this slough, which crosses the road here at this culvert. Now look at all of that water; how can it go through a common tile, and if we had a tile drain in there where would the outlet be?"

Mr. Allen looked up the slough and saw the sheet of water in the main channel and miniature lakes at irregular distances, all of which must pass by them and on to a larger channel.

"Underdrainage is much different from surface drainage like this," replied he. "In the first place it begins to remove the water as soon as the soil about the drain is full; while, when the open drain is used, the soil must be saturated to the surface before any flows away, and then water from distant fields begins to pour into the main channels, and as the ground everywhere is full, all further accumulations must press into and swell our little slough until it overflows. Soil will take in a great deal of water and if we keep draining it away from the bottom it will take some time, in fact, longer than rains usually continue, to accumulate water enough to make a stream like this one now flowing through this culvert. About the outlet, it looks to me as though you will be obliged to negotiate with your neighbor and continue the drain down to his big ditch. But I'll tell you what you had better do; you send for Camfield, our drainage engineer, at Brooktown, and he will make a survey of the farm and tell you what tile to get and how and where you can get this outlet. It will cost you something, but it will be worth to you many times what it costs."

"More food for thought," commented George as Mr. Allen rode on and left him still in the road looking over the farm and thinking of what had been said. While the difficulties of the work seemed greater, the necessity for draining could not be controverted although he had often been told that he had better let the farm go as it had gone for years past.

A few days after the conversation with Mr. Allen, Mr. Camfield, in answer to George's message, was on the ground ready to make a survey with reference to the drainage capabilities of the farm.

"Now," said George, "I suppose that you know all about this business of tile draining and I want full instructions as to the best way to drain this farm."

The engineer was called set in his way and peculiar; and

many said that he knew nothing but this branch of his profession, so devotedly had he given himself to it. A German
by birth, a scholar in tastes, yet, withal, a practical man in
his profession.

Mr. Camfield quietly shook his head—"I'm not very
rich," he replied, "but I would give five hundred dollars if I
knew all that there is to be known on the subject of tile
drainage. There's no branch of engineering science which
is so little subject to known mathematical rules and formulas
as this. Various principles of natural science and applied
mathematics, united with practical experience enter into and
make up all there is known regarding land drainage. There
may be some men who know all about it, but I confess that
I don't."

"Well, give us the best of what you do know," said
George, "we have a hundred dollars to begin with, and we
want you to tell us the best use to make of it. James will
act as your assistant, and it won't be like him if he don't
ask you a good many questions; I'm sure that I shall do so."

Mr. Camfield set a stake near the center of the slough at
the road fence; then he and James, with a chain one hundred feet long, measured up the slough, setting a stake at
each 500 feet, driving one flush with the surface and setting
another by its side upon which was marked the number of
feet from the point of beginning. Stakes were set at other
places also, as, for instance, points to which other low land,
ponds, and flats must be drained. The recent heavy rains,
the flood water of which had passed off, had left unmistaka-
ble marks as to the natural course the water would take up-

on the surface. With the marks before him our engineer could plan to a considerable extent the drains that would probably be needed, subject, of course, to subsequent investigations. Stakes were set in this manner along the entire length of the slough, and at such other places as seemed desirable.

"The next thing," said the surveyor, "is to find the elevation of these points marked by the stakes; that is, to find how much higher or lower they are than the starting point. We will find that by using the level and target-rod."

They then passed over the ground, taking the levels at each stake; Mr. Camfield taking the notes and making a sketch of the direction of the lines and locating the points by their relation to fences, fields, or other objects; thus making a sketched map of the farm. The excellent instrument used by the surveyor enabled him to take levels in distant parts of the field with sufficient accuracy for estimate purposes.

"This," said the surveyor, in answer to James' question, "is a preliminary survey made for the purpose of deciding upon the best plan to pursue—the fall, length and number of drains; size of tile, where to begin, etc. It is not to work by, but that from which a working plan may be made."

After examining his notes carfully for a few minutes, Mr. Camfield said: "We can't get an outlet here at the fence; we must go down to that large ditch," pointing across the neigbor's field.

"But that land don't belong to us," said James; "that is Mr. Bell's farm."

"Can't help that. We must have our outlet there or we can't drain. Your neighbor's ditch will afford a good outlet for your tile and perhaps he will join you in putting in the drain as it will evidently benefit him considerably."

"What are the results of your survey?" said George, who seeing that the round of the farm had been made, had joined them. "What can we do with the 'flat eighty?'"

"I'll tell you how the case stands," replied the engineer, "you can begin at Mr. Bell's ditch with a depth of $2\frac{1}{2}$ feet, run 300 feet across Mr. Bell's field and 50 feet across the road, making 350 feet to your line, where we can obtain a depth of $3\frac{1}{2}$ feet for the drain. Up to this point we can have a grade of only $1\frac{1}{2}$ inches to 100 feet and 9-inch tile should be used. From the fence upward we can have a grade of $2\frac{1}{2}$ inches per 100 feet for 1,000 feet, and for this distance 8-inch tile should be used. The upper part of the farm has more fall and all of the wet land can be drained into the main without serious difficulty. You see that the principle difficulty is right here at the outlet."

"Wonder if neighbor Bell will object to having his land drained?" said James.

"I presume not," said George, "but it is hard enough to drain one's own land without being obliged to drain that of another. I'll call on Mr. Bell and see if I can make a trade with him about it. You may stake out about 1,200 feet of the main and fix it up ready for the ditchers, Mr. Camfield, and we will try and make a beginning soon. That will probably be as much or more than we can do this spring."

CHAPTER IV.

A TILEMAKER GIVES SOME ADVICE.

The line for the proposed drain was now determined upon. A flag pole was set just inside of the road fence, and another farther up the slough where Mr. Camfield thought best to make another angle in the lines; then, beginning at the outlet, stakes were set at every fifty feet of the line and numbered in order from the place of beginning. Two stakes were used, as described in the preliminary survey, and were set on one side of the center of the drain. This was continued for 1200 feet, after which levels were taken at each stake and from these, Mr. Camfield computed the grade and depth from each stake to the bottom of the drain, marking the latter upon each stake in order. He also took the angles of the lines indicated by the flag poles, so that he might make a record and plat of it. By the time this was done, night was upon them, and he left promising that in a day or two he would send a plat or sketch of the work done that day.

That evening at the supper table, the work was discussed. Like families on many other farms, the events of the day were rehearsed each evening; even the girls, Nellie and Alice, added much by their interesting accounts of school doings. It was acknowledged by all that upon the success of the farm depended their home and the advantages arising from securing a competence. It was of interest to all to know that 320 feet of a large drain must be made upon the land of another in order to secure for themselves the benefits of drainage. An expense of forty dollars for this purpose would make a heavy draw upon their little fund.

"I'll venture that Mr. Bell won't let us make a drain on his land at our own expense, even," said James. "I've heard that he is as obstinate as a mule, and don't believe in tile draining either. There's no use of young fellows like us trying to move him. If he does refuse, we are stuck on our draining, sure."

"I'm going to see him at any rate," said George; perhaps I can convert him on the subject."

George found Mr. Bell at home that evening and soon made known the object of his call. He stated his plans briefly and for the purpose of drawing out Mr. Bell's views said: "Now, Mr. Bell, don't you think it is a good plan to make a start at draining that wet land of ours?"

"No. It won't amount to anything. It might be a good plan to open that old ditch a little, but this tiling business is all bosh. You'll just be throwing away your money. That big ditch of mine gives me all the drainage that I want."

"But would not that three hundred feet of tile drain from our line to your ditch make dry land out of that flat, so that you could raise corn on it?"

"Not a bit of it. I tell you that you may put all of that crockery stuff in the ground that you please, and the water will never get to it."

"Everybody who has tried it says that it will, and that it will keep the land in nice condition to cultivate."

"I don't care if they do. I know better. Some folks are always running after some new fangled thing and praising it to the skies, but they soon come back to the old way of doing things."

"Don't you think that drain we want to put in would help you a little? I feel sure that you can raise corn on that slough patch after we tile it and if so, you can afford to help us with the work a little."

"No, couldn't think of doing anything about it."

"Will you not then give us permission to put the drain through your land at our expense?"

"Well I might. Guess I will. The land is of no value and never will be. You boys seem enterprising, but you are making a mistake by going into this tile business. It'll come out like the Norway oat business or the Cashmere goat speculation. Yes, go ahead, if you think it will do you any good."

"Not a very gracious consent," thought George, "but it is as well as I had reason to expect."

The next day, George and James started with their teams for the Brookton Tile Factory to make a bargain for their supply of tile and to bring home as many as the state of the roads would permit. Mr. Allen had said in answer to George's inquiry that the best of drain tile could be obtained at this factory, which was the reason they proposed to patronize it rather than the factory nearer their farm.

"Three hundred and fifty nine-inch tile," repeated Mr. Dennis, the proprietor, as the boys were making known their wants. "You start out with pretty large tile. Most men call for 3-inch tile when they come here for their first lot."

"Mr. Camfield said we ought to use 9-inch and 8-inch for a part of our main and we are following his instructions," replied James.

"O; ho! Camfield has been out there has he," exclaimed the obliging tile man. "That's all right. I thought that fellow would starve when he came to Brooktown and set himself up as a drainage engineer, but farmers are beginning to appreciate his work. Fact is, I sold some tile two years ago to John Bell; lives somewhere in your neighborhood, I guess; he didn't put 'em in in any sort o' shape and of course they didn't work. Bell has always said since, that tile draining is a failure. So it was, in his case, and two others, neighbors of his, did the same thing. Now, if all those tile had been put in so that they would work, I know I'd sold a heap more tile. Camfield is doing a good thing for me as well as for the farmers and himself. You'll find these tile all right," continued the voluble gentleman as he proceeded to hand the tile into the wagon. "You see they're hard and tough; hear that?" (striking two together), "they ring like a bell. They are true, smooth and full size. They won't scale, either, when they are left out all winter, and are good for a thousand years, wherever you may put them. You al-ways should look out for that point and get tile that will stand freezing, without chipping off and scaling, for you can't always get them in the ground as deep as you would like and besides, if they are laid at ordinary depth, the ground will get dry enough in winter sometimes, so that frost will reach the tile. You don't want a tile to keep scal-ing off every time the frost touches it, or in a few years it will go down, actually dissolve, then where will your drain be?"

The smoking kilns and rumbling machines seemed to indicate that Mr. Dennis was doing a good business. He gave the boys only perfect tile and said that they were tough enough to ride in the wagon all day without any loss from breakage.

As they were about to drive away, Mr. Dennis came out of the office saying, "hold on a minute boys! Here's a little book that I'll give you to help you to understand the subject of farm drainage and to keep you from making such bad mistakes as some have made. I make my new customers a present of one of these. I reckon if I had given John Bell one, I would have made about fifty dollars by it."

"Many thanks," said the boys. "It would have saved us some money, too, if John Bell had not made that mistake with his tile and in that way soured him on tile drainage," thought George.

The farm work of the spring had not yet begun. After the first warm rain, the weather turned suddenly cold, so that little progress was made in preparing the grouud for tillage. The roads were far from being good, but by hard work and perseverance, the boys finally succeeded in getting their supply of tile on the ground, though not all were distributed along the line.

In the meantime, George read carefully the little book which Mr. Dennis had given him, and soon mastered its contents. He began to more fully understand both the theory and practice of draining and to get a well defined idea of the practical details of the work. James looked into the matter as well, and became much interested. They agreed that they had begun right and that if they could continue as well as they had begun, their drainage work would come out all right. There were several practical ditchers in the vicinity, one or two of which, they expected to employ, knowing that they, themselves, would soon be busy with farm work.

Two men presented themselves one morning, announcing that they were experienced ditchers.

"Can you dig a straight ditch, make a good bottom and lay the tile all right?" asked George.

"Bejabers, we niver had no complaint yit. We put in a thousand rods last year. We ditched for a livin' in the ould counthry."

"My ditch is surveyed. Can you work by the survey?"

"Bother the survey. We can work better without one. But then we can work by it if ye want. We can do anything in the ditching line, can't we Mike?" appealing to his comrade.

"Work by the day or rod?" asked George.

"Thirty cints a rod, and ye board us."

"You may try it for half a day, and if you do the work to my satisfaction, you may have the job, but if not, I reserve the right to turn you off without pay."

"All right. If we don't suit ye, ye'll be the first one that's complained."

As George explained the survey and how he wanted the work done, the ditchers listened with apparent indifference and with an air of superior wisdom, as much as to say, "you can't tell us anything about ditching."

About noon George made his appearance at the ditch to note what progress had been made An abundance of wet, black earth was in sight, showing that the sons of Erin had not been idle. A glance at the ditch showed that a worm-like trench had been dug for a hundred feet; the cord with which they started, having been thrown aside and the tough sod cut without special regard to the line as staked out. A few tile had been put in position, which upon measurement, George found were not upon the required grade. Tom, the "boss," was in the bottom shoveling out, leaving a puddled mass of mud behind him instead of a clean, smooth, bottom.

"How'll that suit ye," said Tom.

"Not at all, sir," replied George. "Why don't you cut a clean, straight ditch and lay the tile to grade as you agreed to?"

"That's the way we always ditch, and we never had no complaint. The water will run if the ditch *is* crooked. It'll get out some way if we only get the tile into the ground. O, we're all right," replied this son of the turf. "You're stakes here don't cut no figger."

"Very well, then," said George, "your work is not satisfactory. You may leave the field."

With loud protestations and maledictions, the knights of the spade departed for other fields where they could ditch according to their own notions, and where no complaint would be made. Yet they were less capable than those who would willingly employ them and accept as good work that which is faulty in every particular. Such ditchers will not learn the difference between good and poor work nor attempt any improvement until farmers who employ them learn the difference themselves and insist on better work.

CHAPTER V.

DRAINAGE BEGUN.

James did not forget his resolve to investigate the hot bed which had so excited his interest at the time of his entertaining conversation with Miss Allen. He had obtained a full description of it from her brother and had become well convinced in his own mind that he could make one. His mother and sisters, he thought, could look after it during the day while he was in the field, and so a good supply of plants could be raised, which, if sold at the usual prices, could not fail to bring a nice little sum. There was nothing of the kind in the neighborhood and good garden plants for transplanting would certainly be sought after.

Thus he reasoned the matter out, but when the "little mother" was consulted she doubted the success of the project. "The Allens," said she, "supply Brooktown with plants but we must depend upon the farmers about us for our market. They use but a small number of plants and usually start them in boxes by the kitchen stove or at some sunny window, and so I'm afraid that our sales will be very small. We must remember that circumstances alter cases. That which proves profitable to one may not be so to others differently situated. But, James, I think we ought to have a good garden, and a small hot bed in which to start our

own plants, would be a great help. We have two old windowsash that would cover one large enough for our purpose.
We had better experiment with that this year. You remember that couplet in the old reader:

> Vessels large may venture more,
> But little boats should keep near shore.

which I think is a good maxim for us."

James never dissented from his mother's judgment, es-
pecially when it appeared as sensible as it did in this case.
He had imbibed the enthusiasm of the Allens without considering the question in all its bearings. A very common
mistake to youth, and yet it is often what gives snap and
enterprise to many an undertaking that the more careful
and conservative would not venture upon.

With the two windowsash and some old boards James
made a frame, or box, higher on one side than the other so
that the sash when fitted to the top would have sufficient
slope to turn off the water. The frame thus made was ten
inches high on the lower side and eighteen inches high on
the upper side without bottom and so light that it could be
stored under cover when not desired for use. Then he
made a bed of well forked stable manure about two feet
deep and a foot larger each way than the frame he had
made. He now placed the frame directly upon the manure
and filled it to the depth of nine inches with good soil.
After a few days had elapsed the heat arising from the fer-
menting of the manure so warmed the soil that the bed was
ready for planting.

As James and his mother were seeding the new bed, who should walk into the garden but Uncle John.

"Why, Uncle John, where have you been? We haven't seen you for a long time. Have you been sick?" exclaimed James, so glad to see his old friend that he could hardly wait for an answer to the questions he asked in rapid succession.

"No, I've not been sick," replied Uncle John, slowly walking around the newly constructed hot bed, as if measuring its capacity and expense. "Iv'e been out West for a few weeks looking round. I had a little money to invest and thought may be I might strike something good out there, but I didn't see anything that just suited me. There's plenty of land there and if a man wanted to buy some and wait until the enterprise of other people reached out towards it and brings a purchaser, why I guess it will pay. I don't want to spread my money over so much country and wait so long for an uncertain return. I have made up my mind that I can use some of my money on my own farm and make it pay me a profit that will suit me better than to buy wild lands in the West. If I were young and could take my capital with me and work with it, why it might do. I want my money and work to help each other; I have no taste for speculating."

"How are you getting on with the farm business?" asked Uncle John, after delivering his views on money investments.

"Oh, finely," replied James. "We're going to put a drain through the big slough, plow up the old pasture and plant it to corn. Raise staving corn, won't it?"

"Yes, all it needs is draining and good cultivation. Now that I am at home again, you'll see my tracks on the farm occasionally."

After George's failure to get satisfactory work done by the traveling ditchers whom he had discharged, he was at a loss how to proceed. It was now time to do the early spring seeding; and as James had told Uncle John, he wanted to plant corn upon the field through which the drain was to pass. Was there not a ditcher who could do a neat workmanlike job, or had he formed such a high idea of what good work was that it could not be attained. From the lessons which he had learned from his little manual on draining, he thought he understood how important it was that every detail should be perfect.

Two other men made their appearance one morning tools in hand, saying that Mr. Camfield had sent them with his endorsement and recommendations, which they produced.

"I've discharged one set," said George, "because they persisted in doing work according to their own ideas instead of mine. I want this work done neatly and accurately. That is what this survey is for—a guide for the work."

The men stated that they did not work by guess, but by rule and line, and were willing to take the contract on the same terms and conditions as their predecessors.

They accordingly began, George remaining for a time to witness the work. They first drew a cord near the survey stakes and dressed up the ditch already dug until it was straight. Then a line was set according to the marks upon the stakes so that the bottom could be accurately graded. They then proceeded cutting a clean, straight ditch, throwing the soil on one side and the clay on the other. The "boss" cleaned the bottom of the ditch without placing his feet in it, so that in this firm clay the floor of the ditch was left clean and smooth.

At night when George made his appearance to inspect the work he found about two hundred and fifty feet of drain laid, but still uncovered, the tile showing their red heads, so to speak; all in perfect line and dress like trained soldiery. A stream of muddy water was flowing steadily from the outlet, and gurgling down the bank into the larger and clearer stream.

"Tile *can* be laid right," soliloquized George. "My idea can be reached; theory can be put into practice."

"That work is all right, Anthony," said he to the boss. "I see that you are holding the water back in the old channel by means of that sod dam. How would it do to open up to-night and let the water pass off through and over this line of tile."

"I had better blind them with about four inches of clay first," replied Anthony. "If I do not the water will raise the tile and they will not all settle back in position; but if I blind them and plug the upper end the water may flow down over the top without injury, for it will soon settle away and pass off through the drain."

The work proceeded satisfactorily for several days. The ditch was completed each day as far as it was opened, so there was no risk from injury by rains which might occur during the night. As is usually the case with such land, the wet slough, with some adjoining land, had been fenced and used for a general pasture, or perhaps, more strictly speaking, for a range, as the grass had nearly all been tramped out and for feeding purposes it was nearly worthless. As the ditch was open through this pasture George examined the soil closely, and saw that a few inches of the surface appeared tough and waxy, while that below was porous. The water could be seen trickling from the sides of the newly opened ditch, while upon the surface quite near by, the water stood in puddles for several days.

"How do you account for that?" asked George of Uncle John, to whom he pointed out these things. It was no uncommon sight to see the old gentleman somewhere on the Lewis farm a while during each day.

"O; that is made waxy-like by the cattle and hogs having tramped it so much while it was wet. It will be sometime before that works up just right. It takes sun and rain and tearing up to bring that surface soil into shape. You had better leave this lot as long as you can before you plough it up, so that the drain can do its best at drawing the water off. The soil is so rich that the corn will grow and get ripe, if you don't plant it very early. Don't stir the soil while it is wet."

"Don't stir the soil while it is wet," thought George. Had he not done that in the seeding of his oats which he had just finished? Was it not what all of his neighbors were doing every day? Was it possible that farmers o this black, mucky soil would ever be able to obey Uncle

John's injunction? Yet George now remembered having read in the "Farmer" something about the evils arising from working the soil while it was wet. "Guess we must do it, or else drain," was the conclusion to which George was forced.

CHAPTER VI.

MR. CAMFIELD'S NOTIONS ABOUT DITCHES.

How quickly time appears to fly when mind and hands are busily employed with interesting work. It seemed but a short time to the Lewis family since that evening when they had discussed among themselves whether they should abandon the farm or take their chances of success for another year or two.

It was now in the following month of August. The hay and grain crop had been harvested, but not without much hard work and some vexations, in which the ingenuity and skill of James had not come amiss. The corn was developing ears that promised a good harvest. The thrift and good judgment of the "little mother" in connection with the energy and faithfulness of the children had contributed very largely to the success of the summer's work. The garden and poultry yard had been managed by herself and the two girls and had supplied the table with wholesome food; while the surplus of the poultry yard and dairy purchased the necessary groceries for family use. The experimental hot bed had proved a success in that they had early vegetables two weeks in advance of their neighbors, which, aside from being a luxury, took the place of more costly food.

The amount saved in the living expense of a family by the products of a well cared for garden is not fully appreciated until that family is deprived of that important accessory. Mrs. Lewis, who had lived in the city and provided those things from her purse, understood and appreciated this difference between city and country. As the reader may have already surmised, there was not a great deal of time and attention given to house-keeping. Plain wholesome living was all that had been attempted. As time had permitted, James had added repairs and conveniences to the house and barn, while George had maintained a look of neatness and thrift by the timely use of the scythe and hoe in clipping the grass and cleaning of the fence corners.

The main object, however, had been to make the most out of the farm crops. Oats and rye had done well with the exception of about one-fourth of the land seeded, which, because of its wet condition had yielded but little, thereby cutting down the average yield and as the boys thought, the profits of the crop. The hay crop was similar with respect to its productiveness, while about twenty acres of the farm was entirely waste land, no attempt being made to cultivate it.

The pride of the farm was the corn field on the drained pasture lot. The drain had been completed as far as contemplated, and the field left as long as possible before it was ploughed and prepared for the crop. The fact that the sod had previously been nearly tramped out of existence made the breaking and cultivation of the field much easier and the growth of the crop more uniform than it otherwise would have been. George had ploughed the rough wild sod at the upper end of the drain which passed without the pasture and found that it was so rough and raw that he seeded it to Hungarian. Like a careful agriculturist as he was attempting to be, he made a note of this. He saw that wild slough sod land, newly drained and broken in the spring was not suited for the growth of corn which requires a well prepared soil full of available plant food.

"Fine crop of corn that," remarked Uncle John to Mr. Bell as the two neighbors chanced to meet at the road culvert which commanded a good view of the field under consideration. "Guess that will yield seventy-five bushels straight through if nothing happens to it before it ripens."

"Yes, it is fair," observed the neighbor, knocking the ashes out of his pipe and proceeding to refill that important piece of personal property. "But then that is a rich piece of ground, been in pasture a number of years, you know, besides this has been a favorable season—not very wet, you know; shouldn't wonder if the boys would have got about as good corn if they had left that tile out."

Uncle John shook his head. "Yes, that is a good piece of land and so is the rest of the farm, but it won't amount to much without drainin'. The boys have corn in the back part of the farm which I don't think will bring more than thirty bushels an acre and I know that they gave it as much care as they did this field, so there's 45 bushels an acre difference which I put down principally to the credit

of that tile drain. I tell you, neighbor, it pays on land like
that."

"Well, I dun no, we'll wait till the corn is cribbed. This
may not turn out as well as it looks."

"I see you have broken up that patch the boys drained.
for you," said Uncle John, turning and looking on the op-
posite side of the road.

"Yes, thought I would plough it up, it seemed pretty
dry, and as my boys were out of work one day I told them
they might try their plows on it, maybe it would pay and
maybe not. My boys call it the Lewis patch. I go on the
'cut and try' rule, if that patch turns out any good I'll make
it right with the boys about the drainin'."

It may be somewhat surprising to many who read this
account that one line of tile through this slough should have
made such change in this field, for it is often thought necessary to put drains in much more frequently in order to secure such drainage as is here described. The explanation
lies in the nature of the soil and subsoil and in the slope of
the surface. Much of the flat prairie land has a porous
structure, so that if the water is removed from a low place ;
as for instance, a pond or slough, the resistance of the soil
is so slight that drainage water from some distance either
side readily flows through the soil towards such depressions,
sometimes favorably affecting land twenty rods distant
from the drain. This state of things, of course, necessitates
the use of large tile. If, as is sometimes the case, the soil
becomes a little too wet from want of more thorough drainage, the Illinois farmer is content to wait a day or two for

the land to resume its desired condition rather than incur
the expense of more frequent drainage.

The contrast between the drained and the undrained
fields increased the desire of the Lewis boys to continue
their drainage work. They counted up the probable
proceeds from the year's work and concluded that they
could continue their main drain a little farther and supple-
ment it with some branch lines, the whole involving an expense of another hundred dollars. Accordingly Mr. Camfield was again called, preparatory to more drainage.

"I am greatly obliged to you, Mr. Camfield," said George,
for sending me such excellent workmen;" and he related
his experience with the two sets of men.

"The ditching business is like every other," said the surveyor. "There are all grades of workmen engaged in it,
each one thinking his services worth as much as the best,
and acknowledge no equal in point of excellent work. And
yet tile ditching is work that requires skill as well as strength,
and deserves good remuneration when well done. Those
who do not do good work should be kept out of the field.
But I suppose that no amount of lecturing will help the
matter any, for many farmers who employ ditchers must
learn what good work is by dear experience. The persistence with which the average ditcher insists that he is doing
the best possible work is generally sufficient to persuade
his employer that he is, indeed, a model ditcher and tile
layer, and yet the farmer may be as surely humbugged as
he is when within the clutches of the oily-tongued lightning
rod man. Ditching machines are being introduced in some

localities with acknowledged success, the effect of which will be, I think, to lessen the number of incompetent ditchers and secure to the farming community a better class of work. I sometimes think," continued he as he proceeded to set up his instrument, preparatory to taking some levels, "that what the facetious Barnum says about all men is certainly true about farmers—they like to be humbugged; but then people tell me that I look through a glass all the time and see things differently from other folks, so you must make due allowance for my erratic views."

The Brooktown tile factory was again visited by the boys for their supply of tile for fall use.

"Seven-inch tile with which to continue our main," announced George as the affable Mr. Dennis made his appearance.

"More tile is it? I thought you would be back again. This way," said he leading the way to the tile yard. "I never knew a man in this country who began right with his draining who didn't continue until he got his land pretty well drained out. It beats all, the way a little thing spoils the sale of tile. There was Jacob Bass over near H—— who bought some of their tile and left them out all winter. I suppose I ought not to tell this but it's a fact, nevertheless, that those tile actually melted. In the spring there were not ten out of a hundred that were worth using. Bass wouldn't buy another tile at H——, and I can't prevail upon him to buy of me, though I tell him that for every tile that fails I'll give him a hundred. 'It's no use,' he says, 'can't risk any more money in tile.'"

"How do you manage to sell so many tile?" asked George, "You seem to dispose of more than any other dealer for miles around."

"I have only two maxims. I teach farmers in every way I can how to use them so as to get their best results, and then sell them a tile that I know is perfect in every respect. This is my only business card. There is a pile of tile over there that is poorly burned. I've had twenty chances to sell them at a little discount but I will not let one of them go, because they are a poor article. There is too much risk in their use. I'll burn some of the best over again and the rest I'll break up—put them where they won't tempt any body."

The boys thus far had been fortunate in their agricultural teachers. There is one advantage which the student of agricultural books has over the illiterate and that is, he is able to recognize that which is sound in the practice about him and also in the counsel of those with whom he comes in contact. The details given in those books may not always be such as can be followed minutely in every case, but the principles are correct, and so the learner is able to draw the line in the practice about him and say, "*This* looks reasonable because it conforms to correct principles; *that* must be discarded because it is not in accordance with those principles.

CHAPTER VII.

A SERIOUS DIFFICULTY ENCOUNTERED

George secured the same ditchers who had served him so well the spring before, and the work proceeded with the old time care and thoroughness. It may be asked why the boys did not do the work themselves, instead of employing professional diggers. This they had, in fact, intended to do, but after trying the work half a day found that they did not have the skill or strength to continue the work profitably. One man trained to the work would do more in a day than both of them; besides as the "little mother" counciled them, the regular farm work was enough to occupy their whole time and was also more adapted to their strength. While the farmer may not always be able to perform, either in whole or in part, the work which is necessary to be done, yet he may and should know how it should be done, and when it is well done.

The work was carried on with less difficulty and expense than in the spring. The road was now good for hauling tile from the factory to the farm, the ground in the field was firm enough so that the tile could be distributed in place without extra handling. The soil was in better condition for digging and the filling in of the ditches was much easier and more rapidly done. The survey did away with the necessity of having water to grade by.

The enterprise of the boys had attracted some attention from the neighboring farmers. The success of the drained

slough had excited the curiosity of some of the inquisitive
ones, so that it was not an uncommon occurrence to see
other neighbors besides Uncle John watching the operations
on the Lewis farm. One was Caleb Ewing, a man formerly
from New York State, but now owning a 160-acre farm
only a half a mile away. He had spent four years on the
Illinois farm and was known as an intelligent Yankee who
adhered quite closely to his Eastern notions and practices.

This gentleman made his appearance one afternoon just
as the men were finishing one of the side drains in which
4-inch tile had been used.

"I must say," said he, addressing Anthony, the boss
ditcher, "that you do ditching here differently from what
they do back East. I have known every since 1 came
West that this land ought to be drained but to do it the
way they do East makes it so expensive that I did not dare
try it. They put their drains about forty feet apart all
over the field. That means the investment of some money
when a man has 160 acres. I haven't planted a single tile
yet."

"There's a power o' difference between ditching here and
in New York," said Anthony; "I worked there before I
came to Illinois. This soil is more porous than that and
digs a sight easier, too. They don't use so big tile back
there. The water don't seem to get out of the soil as fast
as it does out of this.

"I never knew of ditches being staked out by a surveyor,"
said Mr. Ewing, "they would think that was all foolishness."

"They always had plenty of fall where I worked," replied

Anthony. "I put in some drains for one of the best farmers back East, who used to say to me, 'Anthony dig your
ditch from beginning to end when there is water in the
ground and if you get the bottom so that the water forms a
good current all the way, put your tile in and I'll risk it,'
but then a forty-acre lot is the largest field I ever saw
drained till I came West. The first job I did after I came
West was some ditching for a man who worked according to
eastern plans, and it was allmost a failure too. He used a
four-inch-tile for the main to drain thirty-eight acres. He
had no survey made and though I did as well as I could,
I've always been ashamed of that job. I don't ditch any-
where now unless I have a survey to guide me."

"Are these all of the tools you use?" asked Mr. Ewing,
looking about and seeing only a few.

"Yes, a ditching spade, tile spade, each twenty inches
long, a round pointed shovel, a cleaning hoe, a line, a measuring guage and hatchet. For large tile I use only one of
the spades, the ditching spade. I get the best tools and
keep them in first-class condition. Some men leave their
spades out in the weather all through the digging season,
but I find that I can make twenty-five cents a day more by
simply keeping my spades in good shape; can do more
work and do it easier, you see."

"Just so. Well, I've found that we can't farm the same
way we did in York State. When I first came here I
thought I could raise good wheat on my farm but I soon
found that wheat culture was a failure. Some told me that
the soil was too light, and some said that it was too wet, all

I know is that I didn't get any wheat. I'll look around again before long," said Mr. Ewing, as he walked away.

A few days after this our ditchers appeared to be in trouble. They ate their supper one night without offering any comments on the progress of their work, which was contrary to their usual custom. In answer to James' question about the work Anthony replied that they had not got very much done that afternoon, as they were digging in the 6-ft. cut. At dinner the next day they looked more troubled and dejected than ever.

"George, I guess we're beat," announced Anthony at the close of the meal.

"What's the matter," said George, "I thought you never had any trouble with ditch work."

"We've got a bad case on hand now sure. We are working in that 6-ft. cut and have struck quick-sand. We can dig the ditch all right till we come to the last foot of depth, and then the sides cave in as fast as we shovel it out. The few tile we have laid are full of dirt and sand. It runs in at the joints like water and when once there the water slowly seeps away and leaves the drain full of solid material. We've worked at it more than a day now, the best we know how, and can't make any headway."

"That is certainly a bad case," said George, and they all started for the unfortunate drain.

The ditch was being made to drain a troublesome and worthless pond, in order to reach which it must be dug six feet deep for a short distance. When they arrived at the ditch they found a discouraging state of things. The workmen protested that they could do nothing with it. They had not given it up until they were obliged to. It was a waste of work to do anything more there.

"Then take another ditch," said George, at a loss to know what other course to pursue.

He looked at it farther. Instead of the usual pliable clay found at the bottom of the other ditches, here was an unstable, shaking mass, called by the ditchers, quick-sand. To abandon this drain would seriously interfere with the plans for drainage the farm. If the drain could be put through four acres could be reclaimed at very little expense. Who could help him out of this difficulty? Could not Mr. Allen help him? He had often given him valuable advice from his experience. The idea at last came to him, that Mr. Camfield was just the man to tell him how to treat this case. "Yes," soliloquized George, "before I waste anything experimenting with this ditch, I'll get Camfield to look at it and know what he advises about it. He must have seen such cases before." James was accordingly dispatched for the engineer.

It was three days before Mr. Camfield came to examine the ditch. After looking the matter over and listening to the account of the difficulty as given by the ditchers, our surveyor said:

"This troublesome material cannot be called quick-sand. There is no sand in it. It is a very fine clay; so entirely filled with water that it behaves like quick-sand. Look at this," taking up one of the tile that had been in the ditch three days, "the water has oozed away leaving the clay quite firm inside of the tile. You see that if the water can be drawn away from the mass it will become firm clay."

With the help of Anthony and some of his assistants some of the tile were taken up and cleaned, then filled with hay and pressed in to fill the space,

"Now," said Mr. Camfield, " I think if you will wait three or four weeks you will be able to lay the line of tile as you wish. This clay water moves almost as easily as clear water. The course hay in and about the tile will serve as a filter, so that the water will pass away leaving the clay behind. Of course the clay will fill the spaces in the hay but it will not become so solid as if the hay were not there. The object is to drain this underground pond so as to leave the clay firm enough to work. We have now tapped it at one side so that after a time our object will be accomplished. When the tile are once laid and left clean, the clay will remain firm about the tile and no further trouble need be feared.

"But what makes the difference between this clay and the others we have dug through?" asked George. "Last spring we dug in soil and clay that was saturated with water, yet when it became mixed up by working and was permitted to remain quiet, the soil settled to the bottom and the water passed off clear."

"The principle difference is in the fineness of the particles," said the engineer. "Our soil and subsoil, as we usually find them consist of grains of greater or less size. If we should grind these until they become as fine as the particles composing this clay, and then saturate with water, the mixture would act very much like this one that is giving us so much trouble."

This was a phase of the subject that George had not looked into. The natural texture of different soils and the way they behave under varying quantities of water is a subject upon which few, even successful land drainers, have made observations and yet it is a most interesting subject for investigation.

CHAPTER VIII.

CONCLUSION.

Mrs. Lewis was secretly not a little proud of her two boys, not so much on account of their successful work so far, but because of their steady persistence, and sensible view of things. James whom she feared would prove fickle, and perhaps a little wild, was developing a steadiness of purpose that was most gratifying. The isolation from city associates, and necessity for constant work, accompanied with personal responsibility, had a most wholesome effect upon the whole family. The girls soon found that the country school was by no means a bad place to get an education, while the country life and work captivated them by its novelty, and they were soon as interested as the boys.

The drainage work laid out for the present year was completed about November first. After all the ditching had been done except the previously abandonded 6 ft. cut, Anthony was persuded to again try the neglected drain.

Much to his surprise he found the clay firm enough at the bottom to be self-sustaining. The tile that was filled with hay and mud were taken up, cleaned and laid to grade, and the remainder of the ditch dug without difficulty. This opened up the four-acre pond lot, which by the use of several branches of 3-inch tile, was reclaimed from the dominion of the frogs. James plowed all of the waste land as soon as the drains were completed, thereby leaving the heretofore unconqured soil ready for the action of winter frosts and storms. The drainage now done on the farm has reclaimed about twenty acres of land and benefitted twenty acres more. The interest upon the debt had been paid and George had confidentially told his mother that by another fall he thought that they could pay a part of the principal since one-half of the farm was now in condition to produce a paying crop.

The husking of the pasture lot corn field began and proceeded with the dispatch and drive usually seen during the fall of the year on Illinois corn farms. The field had matured its grain usually well, and as the husking drew near its end, the score which James was keeping showed that the yield would be eighty bushels per acre instead of seventy-five as had been guessed by Uncle John earlier in the season.

Neighbor Bell was not blind to what was going on, though he kept his opinion to himself. He saw load after load of corn drawn from the field and shoveled into the plethoric crib by the barn. He walked over the "Lewis patch" on his own side of the road, which, after lying fallow all

summer had been plowed, and now was in excellent condition for next year's crop.

"This drainage business is a good thing, and no mistake,"
thought he. "I suppose that I didn't get my tile put in
right, some way, which is the reason that they were no
good. I'll take 'em up next spring and see if I can't do
better next time. Suppose the Lewis boys don't know th at
I planted tile before they ever thought of doing it. Let's
see! Guess that I can pay the boys about half the cost of
that drain on my land. Yes that's fair. About twenty dollars. I'll call that ten dollars on my share of the expense,
and ten dollars for the lesson. Pretty dear lesson, that, I'll
be bound," and he puffed away at his clay pipe energetically,
as he compared the yield of his own cornfield with that of the
Lewis pasture lot.

Not long after this, the Lewis family were surprised at
receiving a friendly evening call from Mr. Bell. He chatted
with them about the late election news and the various
neighborhood happenings and as he arose to go he said, as
if suddenly recollecting something: "By the way, boys,
I've never paid you my share of that drain expense. Here
are twenty dollars. I've always intended to pay it but have
neglected it until now." Without waiting for a reply he
opened the door and went out.

The boys were surprised enough.

"Some people talk worse than they act," said Mrs. Lewis.

"Another convert to tile drainage," observed James.

The winter came on with its usual rigors, bringing its
distinctive duties to the farmer boys. George had a fine

lot of hogs which he was fattening for the mid-winter market. James was planning to build a new wood-house which should have a work-shop department. Both spent the evenings in useful study or entertaining reading, thus keeping hand and head usefully employed. They had purchased a few of the books recommended at the Farmers' Institute the winter before, and were now widening their field of knowledge. With these books in the house the loafing department of the village store had no attraction for them.

We may but briefly review the work of the next year. The Lewises decided not to drain any more of the farm until the next fall. They had used all their money paying for the draining already done, and, besides, had found that draining in the fall was less expensive.

With the experience of the preceding year the boys felt themselves quite capable of managing the farm, as now improved, in such a way as to make a considerable payment on the farm debt that year; and so directed their efforts in that direction. They noticed that their drained fields were always in good shape for working; that every change in the temperature or additional rain did not produce a corresponding change in the growth of the crops, and that there was no lost time and strength in cultivating.

Neighbors Bell and Ewing each began to drain their farms, following the examples of the Lewis boys in attempting to begin right and work carefully. The boys were fast demonstrating that they were worthy of a place among the best farmers of the neighborhood. They were no longer commisserated on account of their greenness and expected failure in farming, but looked up to as rising agriculturists and worthy of "honorable mention."

Our girls, Nellie and Alice, had decided that there was more profit in poultry management than in any of the work which they and their mother had tried the year before, so it was arranged that Nellie should have special care of the poultry, while Alice and her mother should care for house and garden, assisted when necessary by James, who stood ready to give a hand in garden, field or work-shop. Thus the work was systematized, each department having a supervision, but all working together harmoniously.

Let us look in upon the family at the end of another two years: It is now four years since the time of the family consultation mentioned in our first chapter. The achievements of the last two years have been no less interesting than those already described. The labor and care bestowed upon the farm had given abundant returns. The season which had just closed had been the most satisfactory of all to the boys, for the reason that the drainage of the farm had been completed the year before, and they were able for the first time to cultivate the whole farm. It was also a satisfaction to know that the draining had been well done as was proven by its perfect success during the past year. They were able to make meadow and pasture without having sloughs and ponds dictate where they should be made, as had before been the case. George's account of the expense showed that nearly five hundred dollars had been expended in the drainage of the farm, but having been distributed over a period of three years the expense had not seemed heavy.

If, in looking about, we should see fit to compare the
present appearance of the homestead with that of four years
ago, we should not fail to find a pleasing difference. Not
that there was evidence of the expenditure of much money in
beautifying, but the place had an air of comfort which is the
result of care and attention, in the absence of which the
most costly residence looks dreary.

Nellie, having a decided taste for natural history and
botany, had acquired a great deal of practical knowledge o·
these subjects, and was expecting to spend the next year
study at the State University. It may be said here t·
the amount of knowledge acquired, and the solid study a.
companied by practical work done by the boys and thei
sisters during the last four years, was of more value to them
than the usual college course would have been. It may be
said also, that not all have the will and desire to make ac-
quisitions of this kind in this way.

The "little mother" was thankful that the resolution made
four years ago had been dictated by the Lord, who has
promised to care for the widow and fatherless. While hard
work and no little care had fallen to her lot, she had nothing to complain of. The money with which to make the
last payment upon the farm debt was in the bank awaiting
the maturity of the note. The farm was well stocked
drained and very productive. Her children with all o
their substantial accomplishments, were still filial and obe
dient to the dictates of her best judgment.

We will not attempt to farther follow the fortunes of the
Lewis family, though the way in which the boys continued

to manage the farm would doubtless be interesting to many readers. This is but one of the many examples of successful farm drainage that might be cited for the instruction and encouragement of farmers similarly situated. Many farmers seek unimproved lands in the West, leaving farms behind them from which, were they to imitate the energy displayed by the Lewis boys, they would get better returns for their work and capital than they expect to receive elsewhere. Many farmers are living on land, barely existing, we might more properly say, which is too wet for profit or ealth. To such we say, try draining. Investigate this matter closely. Get the experience and advice of others and then go to work. There is both health and wealth in it if sound judgment and care are exercised from the beginning througout the work.

www.ingramcontent.com/pod-product-compliance
Lightning Source LLC
Chambersburg PA
CBHW031801090426
42739CB00008B/1108